PANTERA
COWBOYS FROM HELL

C000102049

Special thanks to Nick Bowcott and Kim Zide Davis.

Alfred Publishing Co., Inc.
16320 Roscoe Blvd., Suite 100
P.O. Box 10003
Van Nuys, CA 91410-0003
alfred.com

ISBN-10: 0-7390-4260-2
ISBN-13: 978-0-7390-4260-1

CONTENTS

FOREWORD
COWBOYS FROM HELL

When Atco Records unleashed Pantera's aptly named *Cowboys from Hell* album on the unsuspecting metal-loving public in 1990, it may have been the band's major label debut, but it certainly wasn't their first release. In fact, the Texan outfit had released no fewer than four albums prior to this one—all on their own label. That said, *Cowboys from Hell* was the first opportunity the world at large got to hear the band and also the first one that featured the fearsome, metallic beast into which Pantera had evolved.

From the hypnotically catchy yet, heavy, opening riff of the album's title track, to the explosive finale of the aptly named "The Art of Shredding," it was immediately obvious that Pantera was no ordinary band and their guitarist—then going by the handle "Diamond Darrell"—was no run-of-the-mill metal guitarist. Both were clearly destined for greatness, and it didn't take long for that prophecy to come to pass. By the mid-'90s, Pantera were rightly being hailed as the greatest metal band of their generation, and Dimebag Darrell (yep, his nickname evolved!) was rightfully considered by many as being the most significant and influential metal guitarist to have emerged since Edward Van Halen—a player who had a profound influence on Dime. *"His raw spontaneity always lights me up,"* Dime once told me. *"He made me look at the instrument in a different way, man. He made me look at it as a tool you can screw around with rather than something you should always play very carefully and precisely. He proved technical playing can still be aggressive."*

Cowboys from Hell is packed full of the unique mix of musical skills and ingredients that made both the band and their axeman world famous, and also caused them to have a profound influence on all who followed in their trail-blazing wake—and, if truth be told (and admitted!) on many that went before them too. Let's take a quick look at some of them...

Rhythm 'n' Bruise

Cowboys from Hell is a testament to the importance of having great riffs, great arrangements, and killer rhythm chops. It is also proof perfect of the incredibly tight, subconscious rhythmic bond that existed between Dime and his brother Vinnie Paul, Pantera's drummer extraordinaire. *"Well balanced players rip on rhythm as well as lead,"* Dime attests. *"As far as I'm concerned, it's no good being able to wail out smokin' leads if your rhythm chops hug! [Note: "hug" is Dimebonics for "suck" or "stink"!] I've been into rhythm playing since day one, and a lot of that has to do with having a brother who kicks ass on drums. I grew up jamming with Vinnie, and he definitely taught me the importance of timing and playing tight—and that, along with some great chops, is what rhythm playing is all about."*

Of course, great rhythm chops without great riffs are of no value—enter Dime the riff writer from hell. "Like another of his idols, Black Sabbath's Tony Iommi, Dime had the ability to pen riffs that were heavy, memorable, and, dare I say it, melodic, albeit in a twisted sense! From the infectious E minor blues scale riff that is "Cowboys from Hell" (Figure 1) to the disturbing, chromatic descent that opens "Message in Blood," (Figure 2) Dime's riffs are instantly unforgettable.

Figure 1

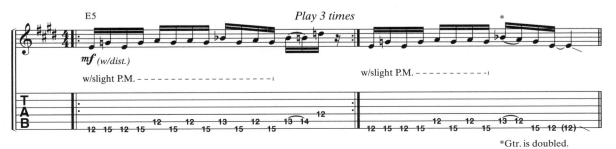

*Gtr. is doubled.

Figure 2

His use of major and minor diads (two-note chords) is also inspired. The verse riff of "The Sleep" (Figure 3) and the pre-chorus of "Message in Blood" are both great examples of this trait in action.

Figure 3

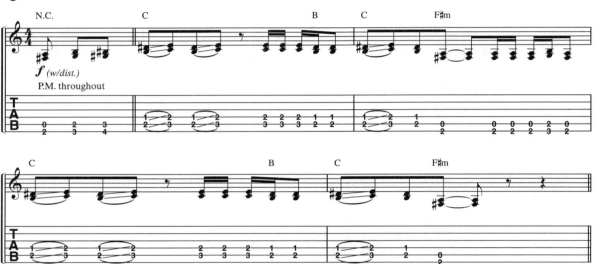

Perhaps Dime's most brilliant rhythm playing gift, though, was his innate ability to make a motif based on a single note both memorable and immediately recognizable. The syncopated, single-note intro riff to "Psycho Holiday" (Figure 4) is a great example of this trait in action—creating a hypnotic rhythmic pulse.

Figure 4

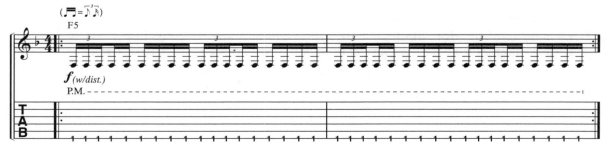

"A lot of Pantera's riffs are tight-assed power grooves like this," he once told me. "In a way, I'm kind of a percussionist when it comes to picking, because a lot of my rhythmic patterns are almost drum patterns...like the beginning of "Psycho Holiday." Only one note (F) is being hit but, you know exactly what the song is thanks to the rhythmic pattern being pounded out."

The Art of Shredding

This entire book could easily be dedicated to the dissection of Dime's lead-playing brilliance! While processing the chops to blaze at the speed of light, like many of his heroes—including Edward Van Halen, Randy Rhoads, Ace Frehley, and Billy Gibbons—Dime instinctively knew when to slow it down and let a handful of well-chosen, well-placed notes do the talking. His restrained, yet remarkably musical openings to his solos in "Cowboys from Hell" and "Cemetary Gates" illustrate this ability to the tee. *"I hate guys who play fast leads all the time just because they can,"* Dime once remarked. *"C'mon, slow down and play some notes that count, dude. Hell, I'll take one note over a million any day! Play that one note with heart, feel, and guts, and then let that sucker sing, just like Billy Gibbons does. Hey, don't get me wrong, I love wailing out leads as much as the next guy BUT only if it complements the track. To me, playing what works best for the song is much more impressive than trying to impress other guitarists by jerking off all over the neck or showing off your new three-handed guitar technique. Tone and feel are much more important."*

When Dime feels the time is right to shred though, boy, does he, and "Cowboys from Hell" is a great showcase of his remarkable abilities in this area. His use of wide stretches and legato (hammer-ons and pull-offs) to create lightning-fast runs while flowing like fluid is world class, as is his note choice, deft use of pinch-harmonics, and superbly controlled, emotive employment of wide bends and vibrato. The inspiration for the wide, fretboard-hand stretches he often does came from Eddie Van Halen: *"I kept seeing pictures in* Guitar World *of him doing big-assed, left-hand finger stretches, and that inspired me to start dicking around with wide-stretch ideas of my own. Another thing I learned from studying those pictures was the importance of my little finger. It's there, so use it—it definitely gives you more reach."*

Another trademark Van Halen trait Dime uses to great effect are symmetrical runs, namely employing the same exact fingering pattern on each string during a run. Figure 5, a run similar to one used near the start of his "Cowboys from Hell" solo, is a perfect illustration of this idea in action. Figure 6 shows a fretboard diagram of the symmetrical fingering used in this lick.

Figure 5

Figure 6

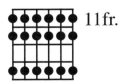

11fr.

I'll let Dime explain how he came up with the above: *"How I came up with this ascending passage was real simple. I was messing around with a wide-stretch lick on the low E string [marked as "initial lick" in Figure 5] and figured, hey, let's see what happens if I take this pattern right across the neck and end on the high E string. I tried it, it sounded cool as shit, and so I used it in my 'Cowboys...' lead. I have absolutely no clue what's happening scale-wise—to me it's just a ripping E minor run that works. I'm into futzing around with symmetrical runs in a major way."*

Harmonic Screams

Perhaps one of Dime's most celebrated techniques is his penchant for using his whammy bar to make natural harmonics literally scream. The first time most of the world heard this was at the end of "Cemetary Gates," where Dime used this technique to duplicate vocalist Phil Anselmo's emotional screams with uncanny accuracy. How does he do this? Once again, I'll let Dime explain: *"I stumbled upon harmonic squeals when I was dicking around one day. A lot of people think I use a harmonizer or a [Digitech] Whammy pedal to do them, but I don't: all I use is my bar and some natural harmonics. To make a harmonic scream, I first dump my Floyd Rose [locking whammy bar system] real quick, hit a harmonic with my left hand while the string is still flapping, and then use the bar to pull it up to the pitch I want. If this sounds complex to you, don't skitz...it's actually a pretty simple thing to do once you've got the technique down. Here's the idea broken down into four easy steps:*

> *Step 1: Flick the string you want to hit the harmonic on with your left (fretboard) hand.*
> *Step 2: Dump the bar down.*
> *Step 3: Lightly tap the harmonic you want with a left-hand finger.*
> *Step 4: Let the whammy bar come back up real smoothly—so the harmonic squeals like a pig!"*

This said, to make matters a little more complex...

1. Dime often does this with those hard-to-hit harmonics that reside between the frets—like the one that can be found about ¼ of the way between the second and third frets on the G string. It's hard to find and needs a lot of distortion to coax out, but when you catch it right, boy does it squeal beautifully! A perfect way to get used to locating those "in-between the frets" harmonics is to master the intro to "Heresy" (Figure 7), which is 100 percent constructed from natural harmonics and includes two of those hard-to-hit ones.

Figure 7

2. Dime often pulls harmonics past their regular pitch—a move that requires fine control over the whammy bar and also calls on you to use your ears as well as your hands to hit the note(s) you're aiming for. To help control this with precision, here's what Darrell does: *"I've found that with the bar aiming towards the back of the guitar [Photo A], I can more accurately get to the note I'm aiming for because I have to push the bar down to get there—think about it! But whenever I'm aiming for a gut-wrenching squeal, I go for it with the bar facing the front [Photo B]. There's a different feel to both, so experiment and find which works best for you. Backward or forward? The choice is yours."*

Photo A

Photo B

The book you are holding was painstakingly and meticulously transcribed by one of the industry's finest and most respective purveyors of this art—Danny Begelman. That said, guitar playing is a deeply personal thing, and the interpretation of another player's work is, and will always be subjective—unless the artist whose work is under the microscope is intimately involved in the process. And, as we all know, sadly that wasn't possible in this case, as Dime is regrettably no longer with us…I know for a fact that if he was, though, he would've poured over every single note! So, while Danny's incredible work serves as the ultimate road map, if you hear something differently or feel more comfortable playing the same notes in a different place on the neck, then go for it! As Dime once said, *"…remember, it's all good, everything goes and there ain't no rules or boundaries. So get off! Tear it a new ass, tear it hard, rip gaping holes in it! Make tracks, leave marks!"*

R.I.P. Dime. Your music, mayhem, mirth, memory and inspiration live on…and always will.

Nick "Hitchcock" Bowcott, July 2007

THE ART OF SHREDDING

Moderately ♩ = 140

Words and Music by
VINCENT PAUL ABBOTT, DARRELL LANCE ABBOTT,
REX ROBERT BROWN and PHILIP HANSEN ANSELMO

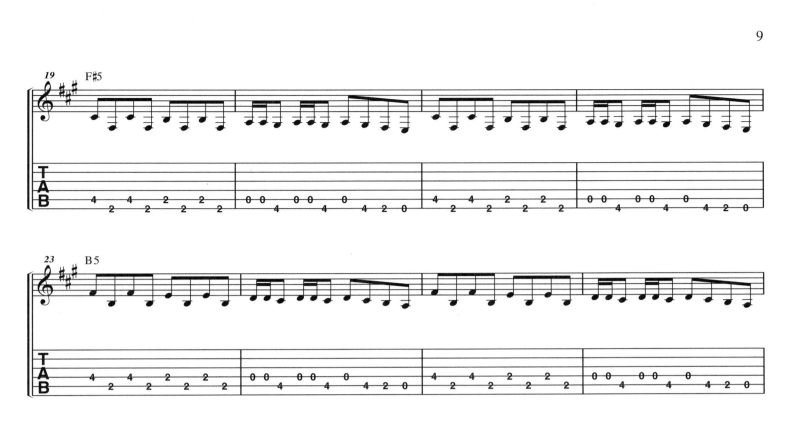

Faster ♩ = 232

Bass & Drums tacet

Play 4 times

Bass & drums enter

w/Rhy. Fig. 1 *(Elec. Gtr. 2) 3 times*

The Art of Shredding - 11 - 2
25955

14

*Chords implied by bass gtr.

CLASH WITH REALITY

Words and Music by
VINCENT PAUL ABBOTT, DARRELL LANCE ABBOTT,
REX ROBERT BROWN and PHILIP HANSEN ANSELMO

Moderately ♩ = 86

Intro:

Drums play dbl.-time feel

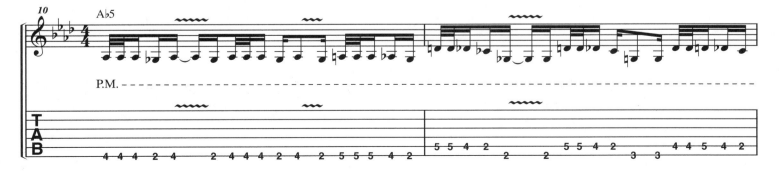

Clash With Reality - 11 - 1
25955

Drums end dbl.-time feel

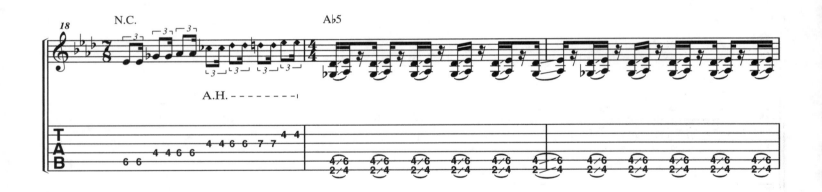

Clash With Reality - 11 - 4
25955

26

*Depress trem. bar to slack.

**Depress trem. bar down approx. 1 1/2 steps

(sounding pitch should be C#).

Clash With Reality - 11 - 8

25955

CEMETERY GATES

Words and Music by
VINCENT PAUL ABBOTT, DARRELL LANCE ABBOTT,
REX ROBERT BROWN and PHILIP HANSEN ANSELMO

Cru - ci - fied__ for__ no sins,__ an im - age be - neath__ me.

Lost with - in my plans__ for life,__ it all__ seems so__ un - real.

I'm a man cut in half__ in this world,__ left in my mis - er - y.__

Cemetery Gates - 14 - 2
25955

Instrumental:

34

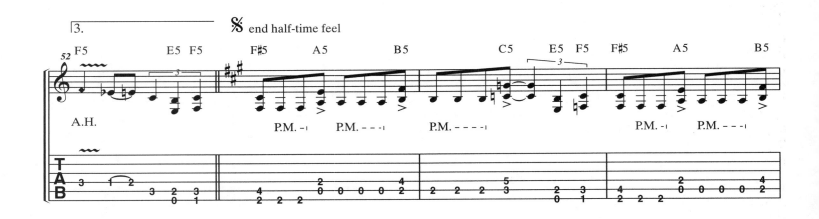

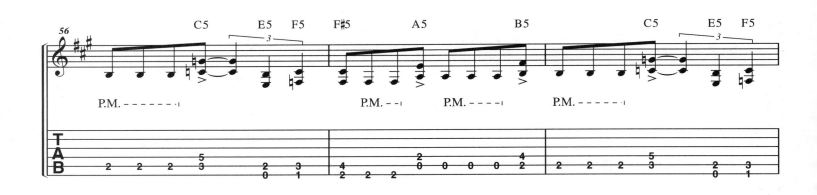

38

41

Cemetery Gates - 14 - 12
25955

Outro:

COWBOYS FROM HELL

Words and Music by
VINCENT PAUL ABBOTT, DARRELL LANCE ABBOTT,
REX ROBERT BROWN and PHILIP HANSEN ANSELMO

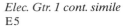

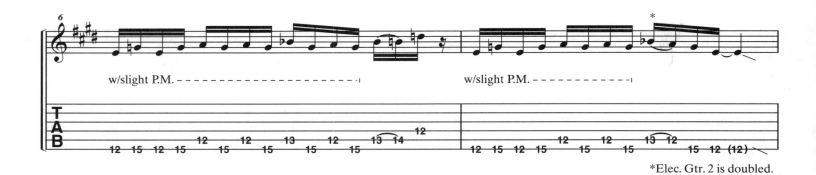

Cowboys From Hell - 10 - 1
25955

52

DOMINATION

Words and Music by
VINCENT PAUL ABBOTT, DARRELL LANCE ABBOTT,
REX ROBERT BROWN and PHILIP HANSEN ANSELMO

Moderately fast ♩ = 134

Intro:
Drums play dbl.-time feel

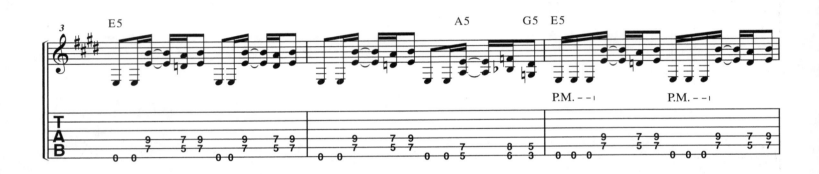

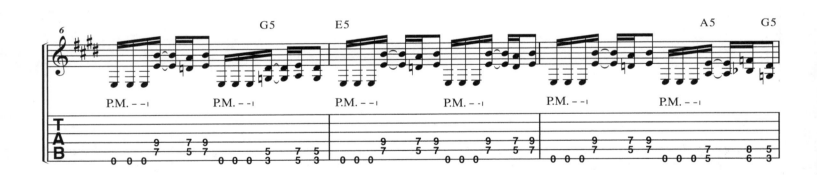

Drums end dbl.-time feel

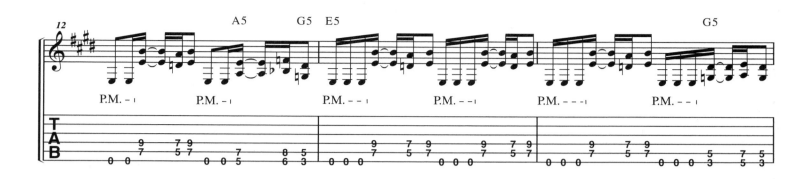

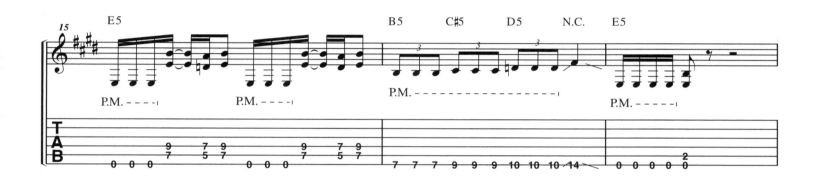

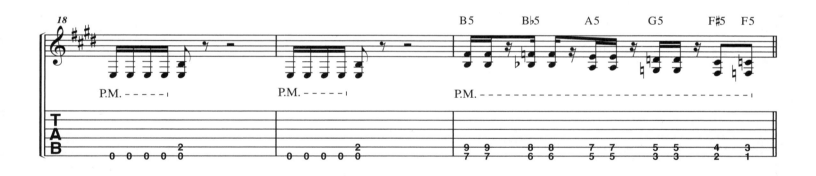

Verse:

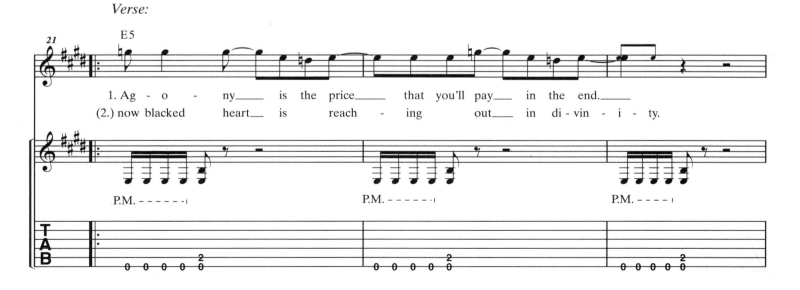

Chorus:
Drums resume dbl.-time feel

Drums end dbl.-time feel

*Depress trem. bar, hit note, then gradually
release bar to normal position and then push in bar to slack.

Domination - 11 - 6
25955

Interlude:

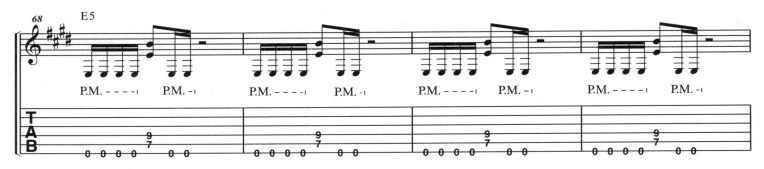

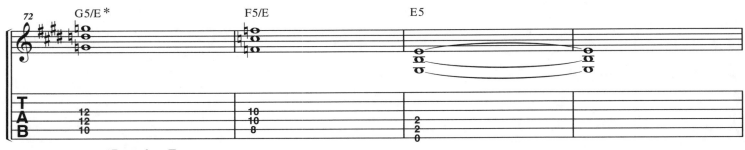

*Bass plays E.

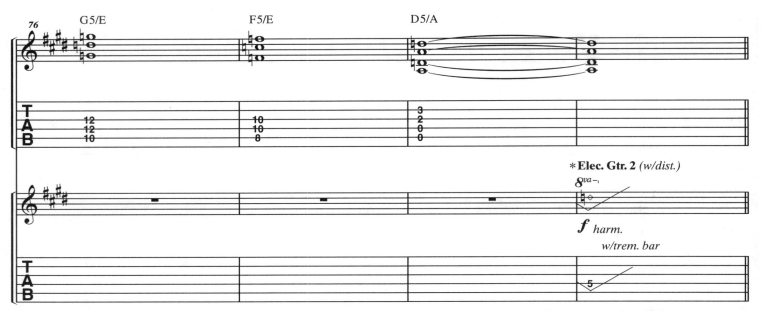

*Depress trem. bar, hit harmonic,
then gradually release bar to normal
position and continue to pull up on bar
beyond normal postion.

Guitar Solo:

Elec. Gtr. 1 tacet

*E5

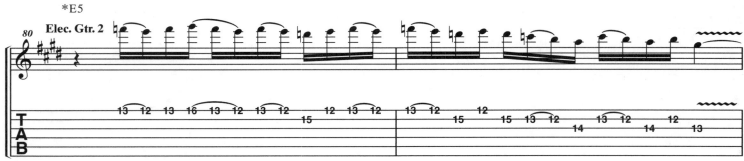

*Chord implied by bass gtr.

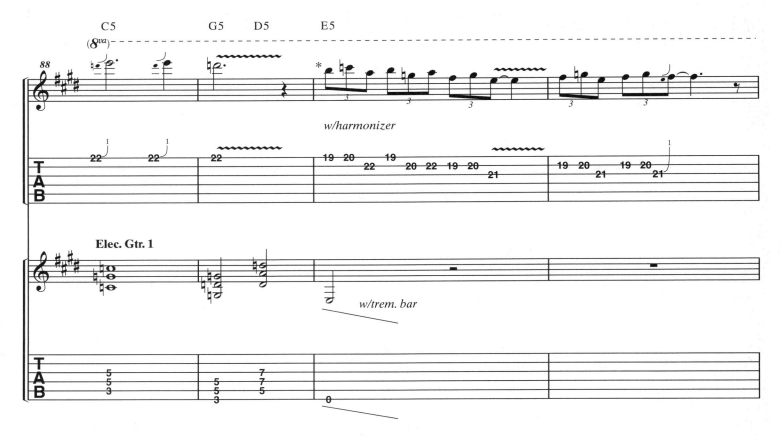

C5   G5   D5   E5

w/harmonizer

w/trem. bar

Elec. Gtr. 1

*Elec. Gtr. 2 played through a harmonizer,
adding the interval of a 5th under
each note being played.

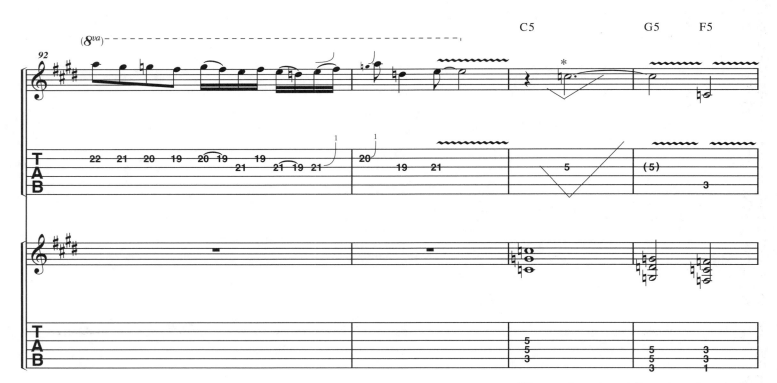

C5   G5   F5

*Depress trem. bar, strike note, and gradually
release bar. Then shake bar for vibrato.

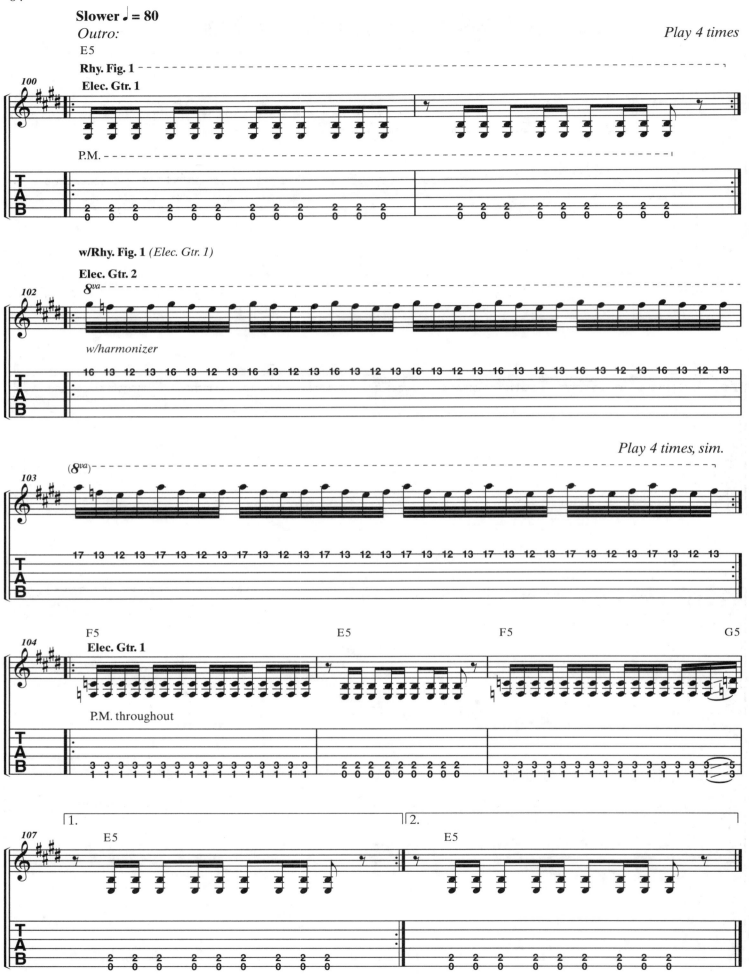

MESSAGE IN BLOOD

Words and Music by
VINCENT PAUL ABBOTT, DARRELL LANCE ABBOTT,
REX ROBERT BROWN and PHILIP HANSEN ANSELMO

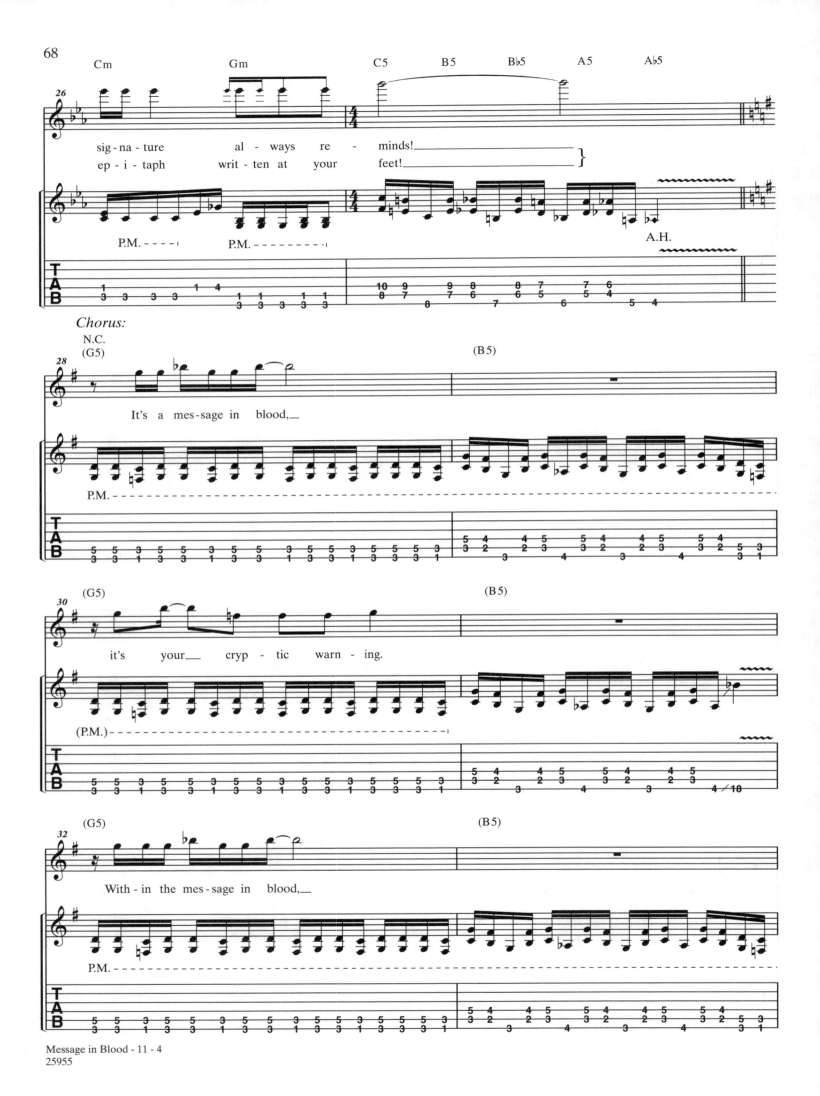

marks the years   of   pain___   and   your   god - for - sak - en   end - ing___

___   to___   life!___

*Chords are implied by bass gtr.

72

Chorus:

It's a mes-sage in blood,—

Mes-sage in blood, mes-sage in blood.__

Mes - sage in blood, mes - sage in blood.____

HERESY

Words and Music by
VINCENT PAUL ABBOTT, DARRELL LANCE ABBOTT,
REX ROBERT BROWN and PHILIP HANSEN ANSELMO

Chorus:

w/Rhy. Fig. 1 (Elec. Gtr. 2) 2 times

Elec. Gtr. 2

Slower ♩ = **168** (drums play dbl.-time feel)

Chorus:

w/Rhy. **Fig. 1** *(Elec. Gtr. 2) 2 times*

Hon - es - ty, born in me.

Her - e - sy!

MEDICINE MAN

All gtrs. in Drop D tuning: ⑥ = D

Moderately ♩ = 96

Words and Music by
VINCENT PAUL ABBOTT, DARRELL LANCE ABBOTT,
REX ROBERT BROWN and PHILIP HANSEN ANSELMO

Medicine Man - 12 - 1
25955

88

Medicine Man - 12 - 3
25955

90

Medicine Man - 12 - 5
25955

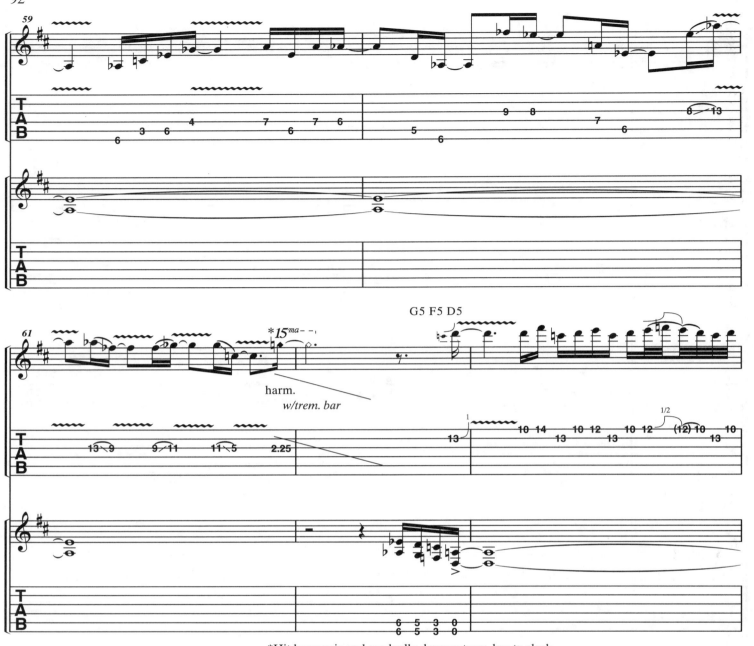

G5 F5 D5

harm.
w/trem. bar

*Hit harmonic and gradually depress trem. bar to slack.

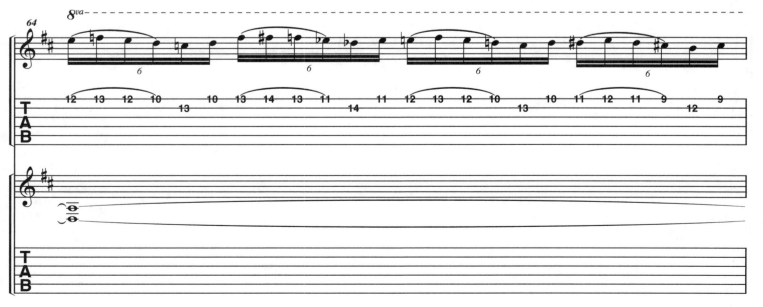

*Shake trem. bar vigorously.

Medicine Man - 12 - 8
25955

Chorus:

w/Rhy. Fig. 2 *(Elec. Gtr. 1)*

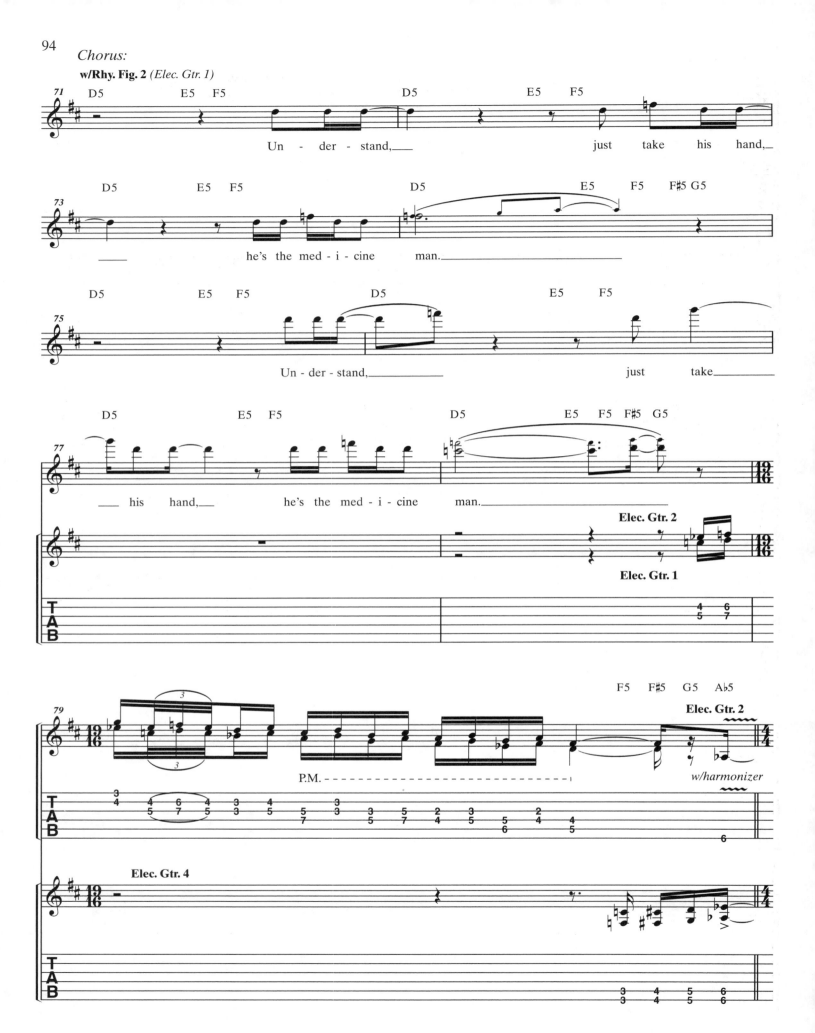

Outro:

G5 F5 D5

*Hit harmonic and then slowly depress trem. bar to slack.

Medicine Man - 12 - 10
25955

*Hit harmonic and then slowly depress trem. bar to slack.

PRIMAL CONCRETE SLEDGE

Words and Music by
VINCENT PAUL ABBOTT, DARRELL LANCE ABBOTT,
REX ROBERT BROWN and PHILIP HANSEN ANSELMO

All gtrs. in Drop D tuning: ⑥ = D

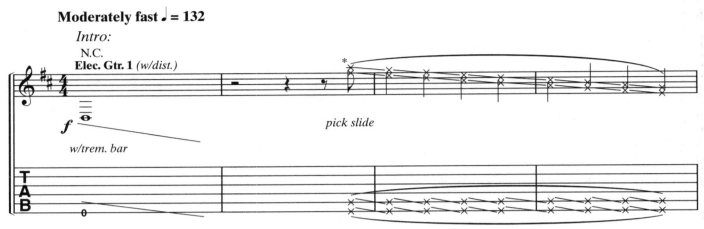

*Begin pick slide at fret 12.

Primal Concrete Sledge - 7 - 1
25955

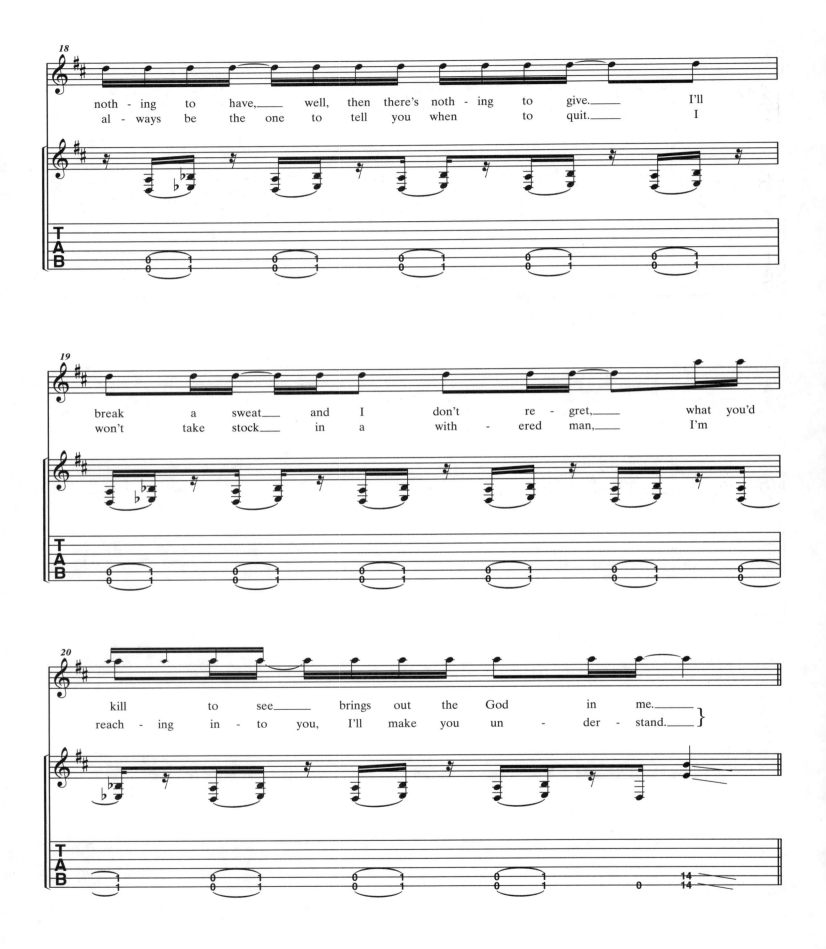

102

104

Primal Concrete Sledge - 7 - 7
25955

SHATTERED

Words and Music by
VINCENT PAUL ABBOTT, DARRELL LANCE ABBOTT,
REX ROBERT BROWN and PHILIP HANSEN ANSELMO

108

Guitar Solo:

*Depress trem. bar, hit note,
release bar to normal position
and then depress bar to slack.

Interlude:

Play 4 times

Pre-chorus:

w/Rhy. Fig. 1 *(Elec. Gtr. 1)*

Freez - ing, there's no heal-

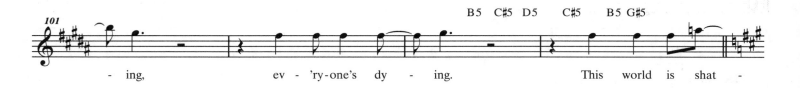

- ing, ev - 'ry-one's dy - ing. This world is shat -

Chorus:

w/Rhy. Fig. 2 *(Elec. Gtr. 1) 4 times*

- tered,_____ all

shat - tered._____ All

Shattered - 11 - 9
25955

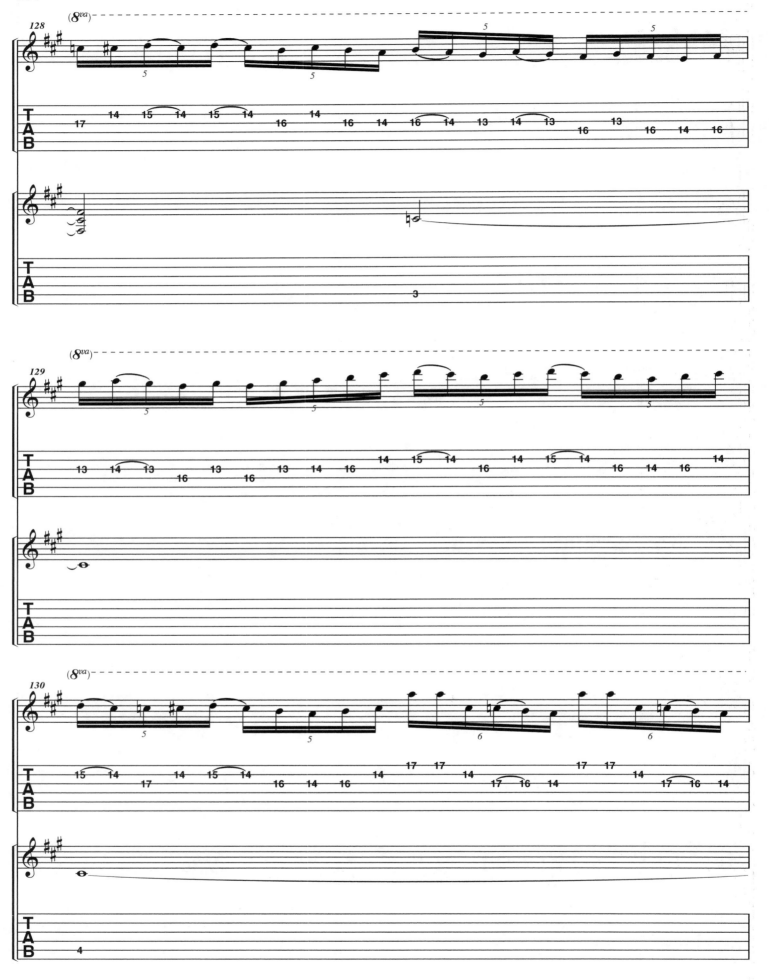

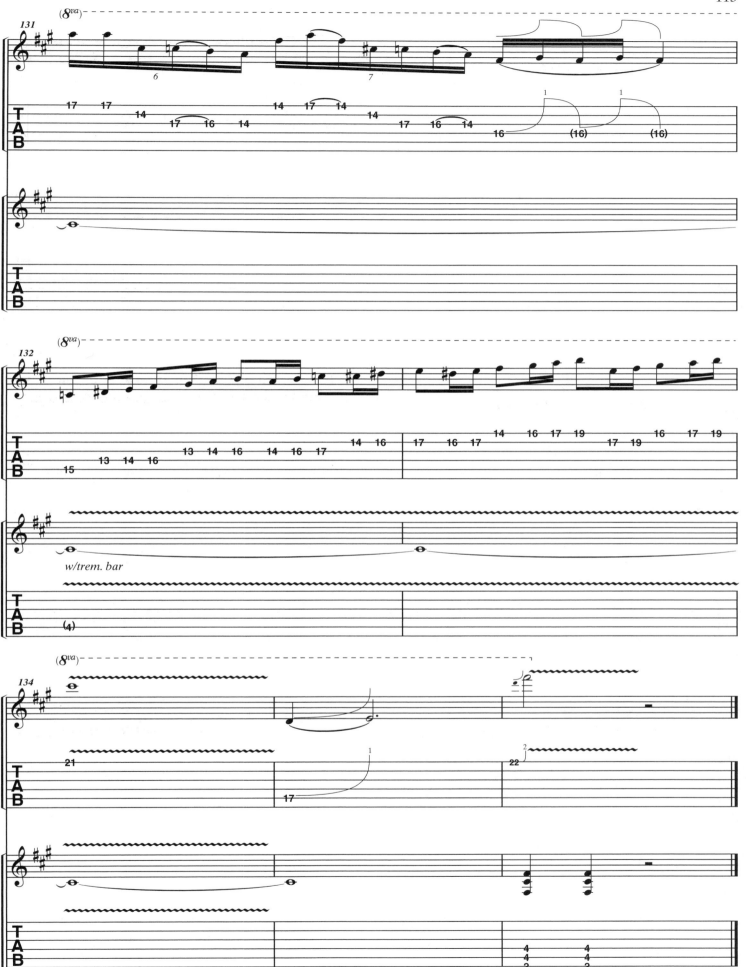

PSYCHO HOLIDAY

Words and Music by
VINCENT PAUL ABBOTT, DARRELL LANCE ABBOTT,
REX ROBERT BROWN and PHILIP HANSEN ANSELMO

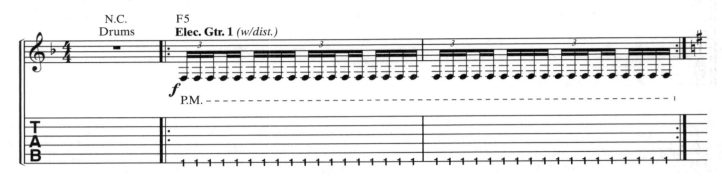

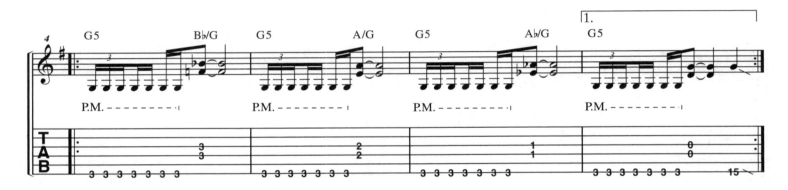

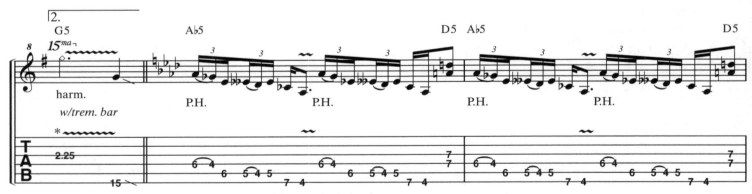

*Harmonic is played a little above the 2nd fret on the 3rd string.
 Vibrato is made w/trem. bar.

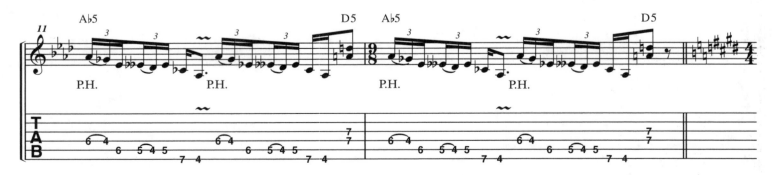

118

Chorus:

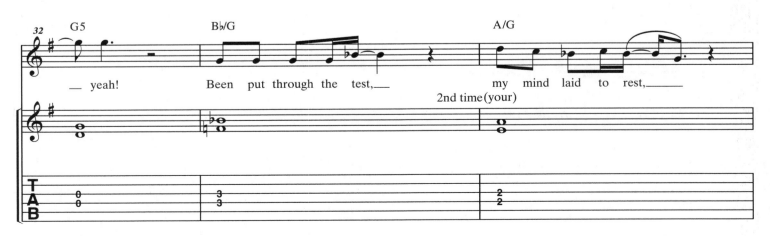

120

*Bend note and then gradually depress trem. bar
in 1/2 step increments.

*Depress trem. bar, hit harmonic, then gradually release bar to normal position.

* Pitch actually sounds one octave higher than played through use of Digitech Whammy ™ pedal (an effect pedal that can raise or lower the pitch by up to two octaves).

Verse 2:
Shot down on sight,
You are the target of attention.
One woman here, another there,
You can't please all the people all the time.
Can't tell the strangers
From the friends you know,
Frustration has taken its control.
(To Chorus:)

Verse 3:
I'm strapped in for life,
Is this where I lived
Or where I died?
You want my money, you take my space,
My mind is telling me to leave this place.
My self insanity has taken its toll,
Frustration has taken its control.
(To Chorus:)

THE SLEEP

Words and Music by
VINCENT PAUL ABBOTT, DARRELL LANCE ABBOTT,
REX ROBERT BROWN and PHILIP HANSEN ANSELMO

The Sleep - 15 - 1
25955

128

Interlude:

w/Rhy. Fig. 1 *(Acous. Gtr.)*

Guitar Solo:

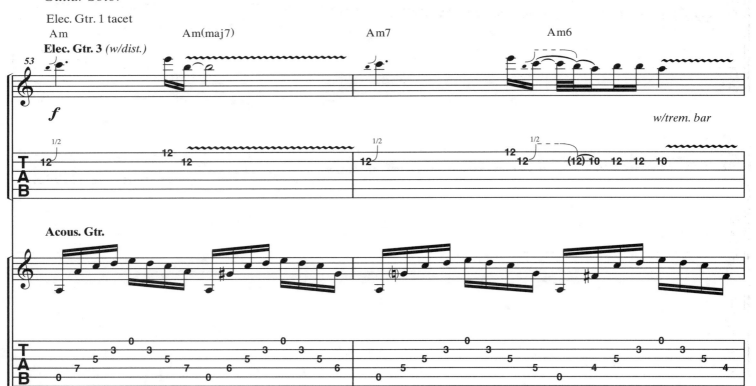

The Sleep - 15 - 5
25955

132   Acous. Gtr. tacet

The Sleep - 15 - 9
25955

*Strike harmonic, pull up on trem. bar 2 1/2 steps, release bar and shake.

134

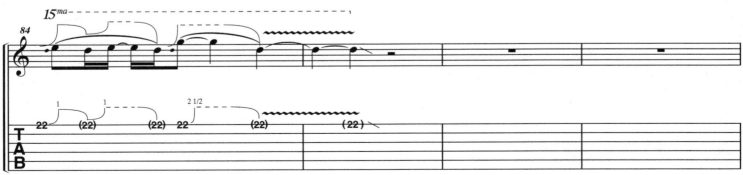

The Sleep - 15 - 11
25955

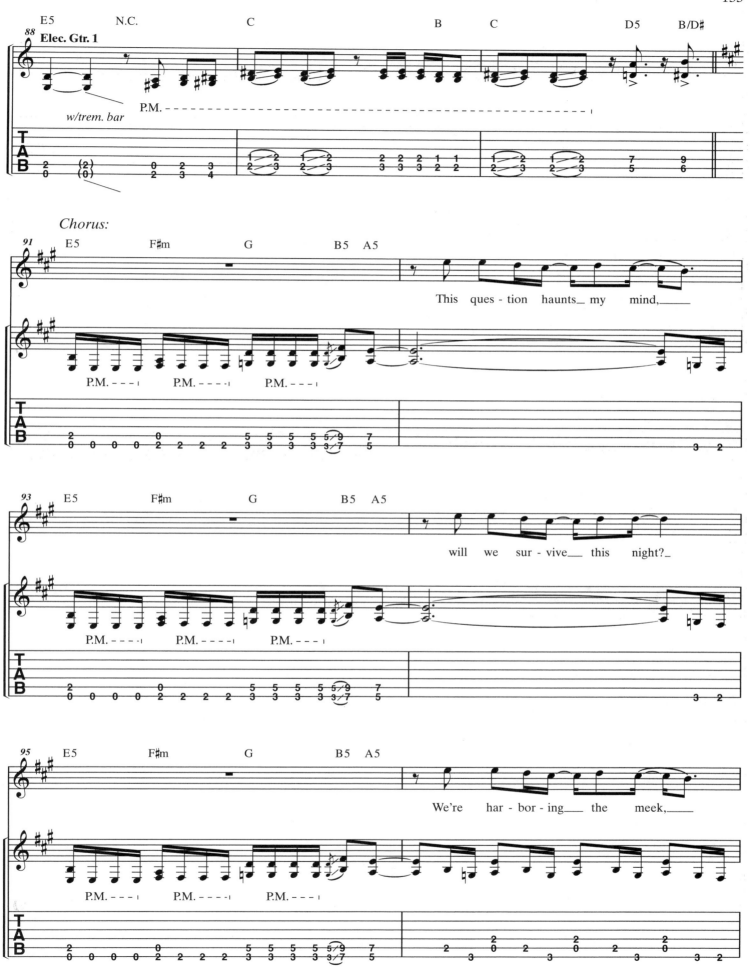

GUITAR TAB GLOSSARY

TABLATURE EXPLANATION
TAB illustrates the six strings of the guitar.
Notes and chords are indicated by the placement of fret numbers on each string.

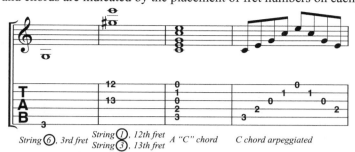

String ⑥, 3rd fret   *String ①, 12th fret*   *String ③, 13th fret*   *A "C" chord*   *C chord arpeggiated*

BENDING NOTES

Half Step:
Play the note and bend string one half step (one fret).

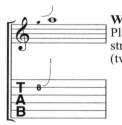

Whole Step:
Play the note and bend string one whole step (two frets).

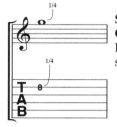

Slight Bend/ Quarter-Tone Bend:
Play the note and bend string sharp.

Prebend (Ghost Bend):
Bend to the specified note before the string is plucked.

Prebend and Release:
Play the already-bent string, then immediately drop it down to the fretted note.

Unison Bends:
Play both notes and immediately bend the lower note to the same pitch as the higher note.

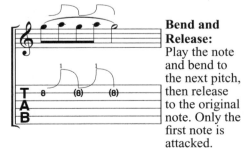

Bend and Release:
Play the note and bend to the next pitch, then release to the original note. Only the first note is attacked.

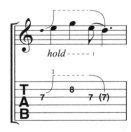

Bends Involving More Than One String:
Play the note and bend the string while playing an additional note on another string. Upon release, relieve the pressure from the additional note allowing the original note to sound alone.

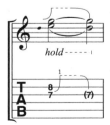

Bends Involving Stationary Notes:
Play both notes and immediately bend the lower note up to pitch. Return as indicated.

ARTICULATIONS

Hammer On:
Play the lower note, then "hammer" your finger to the higher note. Only the first note is plucked.

Pull Off:
Play the higher note with your first finger already in position on the lower note. Pull your finger off the first note with a strong downward motion that plucks the string—sounding the lower note.

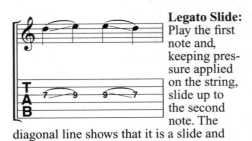

Legato Slide:
Play the first note and, keeping pressure applied on the string, slide up to the second note. The diagonal line shows that it is a slide and not a hammer-on or a pull-off.

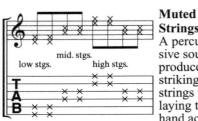

Muted Strings:
A percussive sound is produced by striking the strings while laying the fret hand across them.

Palm Mute:
The notes are muted (muffled) by placing the palm of the pick hand lightly on the strings, just in front of the bridge.

HARMONICS

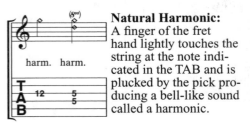

Natural Harmonic:
A finger of the fret hand lightly touches the string at the note indicated in the TAB and is plucked by the pick producing a bell-like sound called a harmonic.

RHYTHM SLASHES

Strum Marks/ Rhythm Slashes:
Strum with the indicated rhythm pattern. Strum marks can be located above the staff or within the staff.

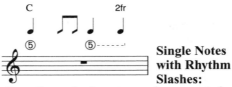

Single Notes with Rhythm Slashes:
Sometimes single notes are incorporated into a strum pattern. The circled number below is the string and the fret number is above.

Artificial Harmonic:
Fret the note at the first TAB number, lightly touch the string at the fret indicated in parens (usually 12 frets higher than the fretted note), then pluck the string with an available finger or your pick.

TREMOLO BAR

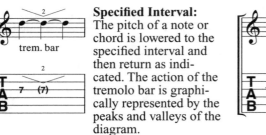

Specified Interval:
The pitch of a note or chord is lowered to the specified interval and then return as indicated. The action of the tremolo bar is graphically represented by the peaks and valleys of the diagram.

Unspecified Interval:
The pitch of a note or chord is lowered, usually very dramatically, until the pitch of the string becomes indeterminate.

PICK DIRECTION

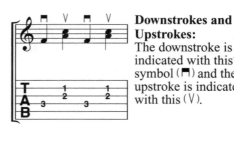

Downstrokes and Upstrokes:
The downstroke is indicated with this symbol (⊓) and the upstroke is indicated with this (∨).